OLD DOGS
NEW POEMS

by

Robert Rahula

ALSO BY ROBERT RAHULA

NOVELS:
Messieurs
Panamaniac
Island of Misfits
Day Another Paradise In
One Last Fling
Bathhouse Stories
Conversation in a Belgian Bar
All the Yage in Reno
Exigent Circumstances
Uninvited Guest
A Modest Summation of Things
To Die in Toledo

SHORT STORIES:
Horror Stories for Children
Behind the Pearly Gates

POETRY:
Trigger Points
Dentro Del Corazón Bloqueada
Camino
Migration
I Sing the Body Politic
Wonderland
From Whose Bourn
Poemas Españoles
Expat Poems

ANTHOLOGIES:
Half Life
The Essential Dan Landes
50 Years Down the Drain

OLD DOGS NEW POEMS

© 2022 by Robert Rahula

All rights reserved. This book or any portion thereof may not be reproduced or used in any manner whatsoever without the express written permission of the author except for the use of brief quotations in a book review.

www.robertrahula.com

This is a work of fiction. Characters, organizations, businesses, products, locales, and events portrayed in this book either are products of the author's imagination or are used fictitiously.

Cover photo: JoJo – best dog in the world.

ISBN 978-1-7329708-9-2

Alma-gator Press
Barcelona • Madrid • La Chorrera

*"O you who turn the wheel and look to windward,
Consider Phlebas, who was once handsome and tall as you."*

-*T.S. Eliot*

TABLE OF CONTENTS

Old Dogs 9
Knots 10
Drunken Angels 11
Getting my Hair Cut 13
Old Fashioned 14
No Wealth Without Liquidity 17
Almost Human 19
Almond Butter Dawn 20
All Those Things 22
People Don't Change 23
It's Hard to Think 24
Is This What It Takes? 26
Getting Forgetful 27
Cruising 28
Victims of Their Own Making 29
Gold 30
Desperate for Love 31
Private Club 32
Evening Paseo in Madrid 33
We Eat our Heroes 35
Magali and the German 36
I Will Miss All That When I'm Gone 39
The Ghost of Mike Moon 40
Tremor 41
Curtis 42
A Very Short Story 43
Advice for Dating Over 50 44
Past its Prime 45
Lost Love 46
Isfet 47
Prayer Cards 48
Consequences 50
Añejo 51
Big Houses are Lonely Places 54

Nobody Knows 56
Time Travel Makes for Painful Lessons 57
Beauty 58
The Only One 59
Giggles 60
Life 61
Opinions and Assholes 62
Waiting for Something 63
Resting on my Laurels 64
What Happened to You? 65
Once in a While 66
Need Overrides Everything 67
Who Would I Tell? 68
Mating Song 69
The Expat Came to Peru 70
The "What I've Learned" Koan 71
Aching to Fly 72
A Friend in Need 73
Free Will...74
Wanton Boys 75
Waiting 76
Gato Viejo, Rata Tierna 78
The Saddest Thing I've Ever Heard 79
The Fuck Poem 80
Just a Dream 81

OLD DOGS

Old dogs like to lie in the sun.
Me, I prefer the shade.
Nonetheless,
I'm an old dog too.
I've been around the block
enough times
that I've gotten used
to being off the leash.

I'm an old dog now,
snoozing in the shade
waiting for dinner
in the microwave,
sipping on a glass of wine
here in the shade,
wondering why I used to wonder
what it all meant.

It doesn't mean anything.
It doesn't mean a goddamn thing.
That's the secret old dogs know.
Now go away.
Don't bother me,
or I'll piss on your leg.

KNOTS

People tie their lives
into convoluted knots.
Everybody does it.
Don't say that you do not.
You spend your whole life running
from the lies your father taught,
only to get married
to a control-freak Lancelot.
You think this is coincidence?
Well... I think not.
Everybody ties their lives
into crazy-making knots.
The patterns of our parents
are the patterns that we're taught.
The evil we rejected
is the evil that we've bought,
hook line and sinker,
even double sinker-shot.
We always tie ourselves
into perfect little knots.
We sign deals we should boycott;
we marry people we should not;
we do things that get us caught;
we spend money we ain't got;
and then we hire lawyers
to undo what we have wrought,
and by the time we hire lawyers
our lives ain't worth a squat
because we've tied it up so perfect
into one big fucked-up knot.

DRUNKEN ANGELS

She was drunk, but then, so was I,
and she leaned in and whispered,
"Do you have my number?"
I said I didn't,
so she gave it to me,
and then pointed at her two friends,
and whispered, "They always try
to cock block me,"
which I took to mean
she might be interested
in some unblocked time with me.
"Text me," she said,
and I promised I would,
and the next day I did,
and the day after that too,
but there was
no response.
Four days later, I got a text:
"Sorry, I was drunk all weekend.
I'll see you at the bar on Thursday."
"Ok," I texted back.

I must have misunderstood
the meaning of her giving me her number.
I must have misunderstood her complaint
about being cock blocked.

When I saw her at the bar
the following Thursday, she came over
and sat next to me,
and after some chitchat, she said,
"I think you and I could really hit it off.
The age thing doesn't bother me,"
she said, referring to the age thing

between us,
that age thing being that
I was older.
"Good," I said, and we sat and talked
and drank some more.
About an hour later, suddenly,
she turned to me and said,
"I wouldn't date you if you
were the last man on earth,"
at which point, I got up,
paid my tab,
and left.

I saw her the following week at the bar.
I smiled and waved, but
I sat and drank with her two friends—
you know, the cock blocking friends...
I found them more interesting.

Some angels drink because they want
to act like devils...
Some angels drink because they're
in pain...
or lonely...
or crazy...
It doesn't really matter.
Women can get away with it
if they're pretty...
Older men, not so much.

GETTING MY HAIR CUT

"So, how are you doing?" I asked her.
"Oh," she said, "I'm doing okay,
but my older sister had an aneurysm burst,
and then when she was in the hospital
she had three strokes,
and then her husband left her.
So, her life is radically different now."
"Wow," I said. "I'm really sorry."
"Yeah, well, my nephew is helping out,
so that's good," she said, and then asked,
"Do you want me to taper the sides up
or keep them the same length?"
"I think a little shorter all the way around,"
I said. "I'm going for a more clean-cut look."

OLD FASHIONED

"There's never been a civilization without alcohol,"
my father used to say.
I was just a boy back then,
so, I could only nod and watch quietly
while he mixed his Old Fashioned.
If I knew then what I know now,
I could have retorted, "No, but there's never
been a jungle tribe, a skid row, or a drunk
without alcohol either."
Of course, he would have back-handed me
for such insolence.

He liked his Old Fashioned cocktail
right when he got home from work.
He took his time in making it just right,
adding the bitters to the sugar cube slowly,
blending in the whiskey with a dash of water,
taking little sips
to make sure it was perfect,
and then going to sit in his big easy chair
with his drink and the evening paper.
I never got to know him well.
He died at 56
walking into the kitchen
to make himself another drink.

We all need our crutches,
great civilizations and jungle tribes alike.
Life mixes the bitters with the sweet
but you still need something—
maybe whiskey—
to numb the ragged edges
and make it all palatable,
or should I say... tolerable.
Maybe it's whiskey for you,
maybe something else.

They say that alcohol was discovered
by monkeys climbing down from the trees
to eat fermented fruit that had fallen
to the ground.
Maybe that's what my father meant:
that alcohol got us out of the trees.
That's about as far as civilization
seems to have gotten—
out of the trees and into the bars.

I come from a family of alcoholics.
Maybe you do too.
We all need something to bring us down
out of the trees.
Maybe it's whiskey for you.
Maybe something else.

My father took early retirement
after a mild heart attack.
He didn't want to retire.
He really loved his job, but he realized
that if he retired on a disability
(because of the heart attack)
that his retirement disability pension
would be tax-free,
which meant he would net more money
than if he worked another ten years
and retired on a full regular pension
which would be taxed.
I watched him do the calculations
over and over at the kitchen table
and shake his head as the reality set in.
He didn't want to retire,
but the math was inescapable.
And so, he retired.
He retired and stayed home
and drank his Old Fashioned cocktails
all day, every day.

That's the thing about time.
Everyone thinks they want free time.
But time isn't free.
It weighs on you if you can't fill it.

My father tried to fill his time.
He worked in the garden,
tinkered around the house,
but mostly he just drank.
He really missed going to his job.

I never knew my father well.
He didn't say much.
He didn't seem to have any close friends.
I remember reading his obituary,
reading about all the things
he had done in his life...
It was like reading about a complete stranger.

I do think he tried
in his own way
to teach me something...
but all I really remember
is how carefully and exactingly
he made his drinks.

I worry that I am like him.
Women worry they will become their mothers,
and men worry they will become their fathers.
It's human nature—we learn by imitation.
Although I don't drink whiskey.
I prefer wine.
But I do like to drink at home
where I can go quietly off to bed
when I've had enough.
I learned that from my father:
Avoid trouble and drink quietly.
I guess I'm old fashioned that way.

NO WEALTH WITHOUT LIQUIDITY

There is no wealth without liquidity.
Think about it.
If you buy a million-dollar house
but can't sell it...
can't sell it at all...
It's been on the market for 7 years,
and you keep marking it down
but nobody's buying...
then are you really wealthy?
If you can't liquidate the house,
then you have no money to buy
anything else.

Or, say you had a million dollars
worth of diamonds,
but the bottom just dropped out
of the diamond market,
and now you can't sell them.
Are you wealthy or do you just
have a handful of rocks?
There's no wealth without liquidity.

There's no true love without divorce.
Without the risk that you might lose
the person you love,
you're just stuck with someone who snores
all night long for the rest of your life.
There's no incentive
to make the marriage work,
to be a better lover,
a better partner,
a better person.
There's no true love without divorce.

There's no true happiness without death.
If you were going to live forever,
you'd would be so bored...
After 1000 years you would have seen
every beach, every mountain...
You would have taken every drug,
every roller coaster,
every exotic tour...
you would be so bored,
you'd want to kill yourself,
except... you wouldn't die.
There's no thrill
no surprise
no joy
no happiness
no life
without death.

There's no wealth without liquidity.
It's not investing that makes us rich.
It's divesting –
divesting ourselves of stuff...
Divesting makes us rich.
Divorce makes us love.
Death makes us live.

Just sayin'.

ALMOST HUMAN

Jesus was almost human, they say...
That's what we are, you know – almost human...
caught halfway between heaven above
and the shit hole of our lives here below.
Never quite getting it right...
Stumbling through life
trying to understand
trying to heal ourselves
trying to write
trying to reach each other
as if we could walk on water
reaching for the stars
and always
always
falling on our face...
There's no real point to it –
this endless horror show...
but we pick ourselves up
and we try again, don't we?
I guess that's the human part in us –
how we try and pick ourselves up
out of these failed marriages
these failed love affairs
these failed friendships
these failed poems...
always searching for that one moment,
that special moment,
like here tonight,
here, right now
when we feel
almost human.

ALMOND BUTTER DAWN

It seems I'm always making lists,
like ways to improve myself
or things I need to buy
or things I need to do so I don't
lose my mind...
For example, today I decided
that I needed to eat dinner out tonight
because if I cooked one more dinner
at home alone
I would feel the walls start to close in,
so I made a list of places I could go,
places a man could go alone
to eat a meal and have a glass of wine
and not feel like he stood out
as a loser for being alone,
and thus I had to rule out most
of the restaurants in town,
but finally decided on one local bar
that serves a good seafood chowder.
It's tough to be an old man in America...
Well, it's okay if you have lots of money...
Then the women seem to find you.
They must have a nose for money.
I shower every day, and yet
I must still smell poor...
But I digress.
I was talking about lists.
I am a bit compulsive about lists –
always making them and then
crossing off each completed item
as if it were a victory...
Well, I suppose it is a victory in one sense...
It's a marker on the road of maintaining...
And so tonight I will go to that bar
and I will sit at that bar

and order a glass of white wine
and a bowl of their seafood chowder
and I will sit there and eat it,
maybe even have a second glass of wine,
and then return to my apartment
somewhat refreshed,
or at least nourished,
and I will open a new bottle of wine
and drink a toast to keeping the walls
where they should be...
Let's see, what else is on my list?
Oh yes, I need to walk downtown
and buy a lottery ticket
and some almond butter
and some Dawn dish soap...

ALL THOSE THINGS

All those bad things I did
so many years ago
or maybe more recently...
anyway, I'm sorry for doing them,
but you know that was then
and this is now
and I don't do those things anymore,
at least not to you...
all those things
all those bad things
so many years ago.

The fire has burned down to coals
so there's still plenty of heat
but not so much flame
not so much flame
all those things
all those bad things.

Soon the coals will burn out
and only ash will remain
ashes to ashes
all those things
all those bad things
so many years ago...

PEOPLE DON'T CHANGE

People don't change.
I've wanted that to not be true for so long,
but it's just a fact.
People don't change.
Your personality is as much a part of you
as your breathing.
You can hold your breath for a minute
or two
but then your lungs demand air
and you gasp it in greedily.
You can hold back your personality
for a week or two,
push it down, disguise it, distract it,
but it will burst through with a vengeance
and an agenda,
greedily manipulating all those around you,
misrepresenting, lying, conning, conniving,
cheating, ghosting, tricking, justifying,
and sucking in the trust and gullibility
of others as if it were oxygen.
I know.
I've watched others.
I know.
I've tried to change myself.
It can't be done.
People don't change.

IT'S HARD TO THINK

When you're a gringo with money,
spending it freely
because everything is so cheap down here,
and you're keeping the local economy alive
and the sun is warm
and the beach is nearby,
it's hard to think that the locals
might hate you as they smile
and hand you your change...

When you're a guy
buying her dinner,
paying for her vacation on the beach,
buying her a new outfit,
paying for the hotel room,
running your hands over her firm young body,
it's hard to think of yourself as a slave owner...

When you're white and successful
and know how to manipulate the markets
so that you get richer every day,
just by sitting back
and letting your money make money for you,
it's hard to think that other cultures
are better off without your investments....

When you've diversified your wealth
as much as you can,
spreading it evenly in stocks, bonds,
index funds, gold, cash, small cap, large cap...
to be as safe as possible...
it's hard to think that one day
it could all simply disappear
with one bomb,
one crash,
one coup,
one conspiracy,
one death,
one event...

When you've spent all your life
thinking through every contingency,
every single possible way
that things could go wrong
so that you have a plan to deal with it,
so that you can safely and securely
navigate through life...
it's hard to think that you might have missed
the one event that will ruin you....

You're no different than the tulip speculator,
the colonialist,
the slave owner....

Corruption is in the marrow of Adam's rib,
and we're all on the take.

IS THIS WHAT IT TAKES?

Do I have to really have to bear my soul?
Do I have to hang on your cross?
Are my scars not enough?
Do I have to make fresh cuts to reach you?
Is this what it takes?
Do you want to rip out my tongue
so I never say the word love
or want or desire or lust?
Do you want to fill my mouth with earth
so your kisses always taste like dirt?
Is this what it takes for me to survive?
Is not being alive what it takes to survive?
To sew my lips shut
to never say I want you?
to push all feelings down
until my heart chokes on its own blood?
I wanted you... but I never wanted this.
I never said I would do this.
I never promised anything.
I just showed up
and then the circus began.
I'm no trapeze artist.
I never wanted to walk the wire
or make the lions submit to my whip
or be shot out of love's cannon.
I never wanted to work
this sideshow of desire,
to drink your Sterno all day
to kill the pain enough
so I could shove needles through my arm all night
and call it love.
This is not love.
This is a cheap burlesque show
And I'm done.
I'm sorry I wasted your time
And I'm sorrier you wasted mine.

GETTING FORGETFUL

I forgot my jacket.
I forgot how cold San José can get
when it's cloudy and the wind blows.
I forgot how cold the buses are
when the AC is on.
I remember the last time
that I took the bus
how glad I was that I had my jacket,
but I forgot it this time
and I'm already at the bus station...
the old bus station...
It'll be a chilly ride down to
Manuel Antonio.
I forgot to tell you
how much I love you.
I remember how good it felt
the last time I said it,
but today I forgot.
I hope I remember to tell you
the next time we talk.
I don't know why I'm so stupid
and forget these obvious things.
It's going to be a chilly ride
down to Manuel Antonio.
You'd think I'd learn.

CRUISING

Would you travel halfway around the world
to have sex?
"No," you say?
"Too much trouble," you say?
Yet millions of people do.
They spend twenty hours in a plane
to walk around the humid streets of Bangkok
looking for a petite Thai girl (or ladyboy)
to fuck...
Or they fly to Amsterdam
"To see the Van Gogh museum," they say,
but their nights are spent cruising
the red light district
looking at each hooker (or ladyboy)
on display in the windows...
Or they drive two hours to "co-ed night"
at the gay bathhouse....
Or they fly to Costa Rica for the "sportfishing"
but never get on a boat...
Or they fly to Vegas "to gamble"
but never go to the casinos...
Or they only stay at gay hotels
when they travel
hoping to meet someone
at the bar or by the pool...
Or they google "sex clubs"
before deciding where to vacation...

Don't tell me you're any different –
you who are getting dressed up
to go downtown "just for a drink."

We're all cruising,
some more aggressively than others,
but we're all cruising.
Believe me, I know.

VICTIMS OF THEIR OWN MAKING

Stepping on the very punji stakes
that they carved,
crying out that they have been wronged
by the fates, by life, or by those people
that they gave sharpened stakes to.
Victims of their own making,
showing you their bloody wounds like
proud tattoos that prove their victimhood.
You see them everywhere:
in line at the US Embassy having lost
their passports for the third time;
In domestic violence court testifying
against the very man they let move in;
Sleeping on the street after
turning down the free bed
at the Salvation Army
so they could be free to drink...

This is our battle cry:
"It's not our fault."

In big mistakes or in small splinters,
we carve our punji sticks and place them
in the path we walk;
We select the nails on which
we will be hung;
We pay the guards who hammer the nails in.

GOLD

The little college asked me to come
and give a one-day seminar
on poetry and creative writing.
I said I don't have time, and besides
I have nothing to say
about poetry and creative writing.
They said we'll pay you $500 plus expenses.
I said I love teaching – when should I arrive?

Now, make a poem out of that.

That's all poetry is, you know.
Finding that little event
that gets trapped in the corners of life,
that little event that symbolizes
how twisted, weird, or beautiful
life really is.

Poems are like these little flakes of gold
swirling all around us in the river of time.
Gold gets trapped under the rocks along the banks
when the river unexpectedly turns course.
Or when the river widens
and the rush of time slows down,
some nuggets will settle into the bedrock.
Some gold is concentrated
in the coarser sediments of society.
Or where two rivers meet with much turbulence,
the complex rotations will spin gold to the edges.
And much gold can still be found in the ancient river beds
where no water even flows anymore.

Poets are prospectors.
We don't write poems.
We find them.

DESPERATE FOR LOVE

When you're desperate for love,
you don't know it.
It's not like the liquor store where
they call you by your name when you walk in.
It's not like the casinos where
the slots scream at you to come and play.
It's not like the whores outside the whore bars
saying, "Hey, come on in, buy me a drink."
It's not like meth when your body says it will kill you
if you don't score.
The absence of love doesn't speak, doesn't scream...
in fact, it barely whispers.
When you're desperate for love, you feel normal.

If you don't drink, you get on edge, irritable, angry.
And if you don't throw the dice, bet the odds, risk money
you can't afford to lose, you don't feel alive.
And if you don't fuck, you feel inhuman, robotic, empty.
And if you don't score, your bones grind at your flesh.
But when you're desperate for love, you feel normal.
It's just one day after another.
Normal.

But when you're desperate for love,
maybe you have an extra glass of wine... or two....
maybe you stop by the casino after work...
maybe you stop by the brothel just to "check things out"...
or maybe you indulge in a little powder diversion...
but that has nothing to do with love, does it?
No sir... nothing to do with love.

When you're desperate for love,
the only thing left are diversions.
When you're desperate for love,
all that's left are addictions.

PRIVATE CLUB

The sign said "Private Club"
and there was a big man standing outside,
but he seemed approachable.
He even smiled when I asked,
"Buenos, habla ingles?"
"Yes," he said, "I speak English."
"What type of private club is this?" I asked.
"It's a whorehouse," he said bluntly.
"Ten Euros entry fee, but that gets you one drink.
We have twenty girls inside. You want to come in?"
I considered it. I know these types of places.
Lots of eager women, usually topless.
Forty Euros to sit in a corner and nuzzle them,
to play with mammets and to tilt at lips,
(as Hotspur said)
while they sweet talk you
into paying a hundred Euros more
to go upstairs for half an hour,
or two hundred Euros for an hour.
I had the money, but I just wasn't horny...
I just wasn't horny...
and at my age, just being curious
doesn't cut it anymore.
"Not right now," I said.
"We close at 6 a.m." he said, and turned away
to scan the street for more willing customers.
I tucked that information away,
but I doubted I'd use it.
I prefer my whores at the beginning of their shift,
when they're not fucked out and worn out by dozens
of old gringos who can't find sex any other way...
gringos like me.

EVENING PASEO IN MADRID

I was in Madrid.
It was evening
and I was walking around the Chueca district,
strolling the streets where the whores work.
I like watching streetwalkers.
I often walk around just to observe them.
It's the market economy in its purist form,
human interaction in its purist form...
Anyway, there was this one whore
standing in the doorway of a closed-down theatre
wearing sunglasses.
The sun had set,
but she had on these huge Greta Garbo sunglasses,
and as I got closer I could see she was old,
maybe as old as me,
way into her sixties
with her wrinkly neck and her dyed-blonde hair
and her huge sunglasses.
"Oye, ven aquí, quiero hablar," she said to me.
I lied and said, "No hablo español."
She switched to English. "Come here."
I paused for just a second.
She grabbed my arm and said,
"It's possible to fuck for twenty-five Euros."
And for a millisecond I considered it.
I considered it because I find taboos exciting,
and the idea of fucking an old dry wrinkly whore
had a certain taboo perversity to it,
a certain "I wonder what that would be like?"
quality to it.
Horror has its own attraction, you know.
But a millisecond is only one thousandth
of a second, and in that millisecond,
I also weighed the risks (disease and otherwise),
and decided it was not worth the risk,
and so I smiled and said, "Thank you, but not tonight,"
and walked away.

I continued my evening stroll and considered
what forces and events would cause an old woman
to turn tricks?
Poverty?
Grandchildren to feed?
A life-long occupation and no other skills?
Or maybe she just likes fucking.
I never understand how people end up doing
what they do with their lives.
Me – I just like walking the streets watching whores.

WE EAT OUR HEROES

They are imprinted on our brains,
our fathers mothers older brothers sisters...
We are such stupid creatures
staring from our cribs
eating every vision we see
taking in every word every gesture
deciding what it is and making it our own.
This is how the world ends – in our beginning.
The parent of the opposite sex tells you what to do
and the parent of the same sex shows you how to do it.
We take it all in and make it our destiny
repeating every sin, every dumb choice, every outcome
of our fathers our fathers' fathers and their fathers,
our mothers our mothers' mothers and their mothers,
all the way back through the centuries
to the first apple tree.
We eat our heroes and dethrone them by becoming them,
making the same mistakes, the same bad choices,
swirling our fingers in the sand making the same patterns,
powerless to stop the biology of consuming information
and becoming what we eat.

MAGALI AND THE GERMAN

The German asked Magali over for a drink,
thinking he was going to get sex,
and Magali assumed it was just
to have a drink,
and chat, as friends might do.

After all, he had always acted friendly,
which is what Germans
(or anyone who wants sex)
might do to get you into their apartment.

So anyway, the German asked her over
for a drink
and they had a drink
or two
and then he started kissing her
which she thought was weird
and then he started to go a bit further
and she said no
because she had only come over for a drink,
but by now it was late
and the buses weren't running
and the subway was dangerous at that hour
so he said, "Well, you can sleep on the couch"
pointing to the loveseat
(which, ironically, had not led to love for him)
but you know how it is,
you can't sleep on a loveseat,
although she tried,
but finally she called a friend
to come pick her up
at 2 a.m. in the morning,
after which she called me
to rant about the insensitive German
who went to sleep in his big bed
leaving her on the tiny couch.

And part of me was sympathetic.
"Damn Germans," I told her.
And part of me was aloof.
"Well, what did you expect?"
And part of me was paternal.
"I'm sorry that happened, but you see,
when a man invites you over to his apartment..."
And part of me was relieved
that she had gotten home safely
and part of me was annoyed
that she had called me at 3:00 in the morning
to rant about how this German had tried to
take advantage of her.

So I asked her if she had to work tomorrow
and she explained that she worked
the second shift (starting at 2 p.m.) so she
was free to talk...

But, she said, she had to work with this other guy
tomorrow that she really liked,
but it was difficult, because they had had sex once
and now he didn't want a relationship,
but they worked together, so she had to see him
every day.
"I see," I said, meaning that I was seeing a pattern.

Sex is the alchemist of everything.
The unseen saboteur, the anarchist, the catalyst,
and the spoiler of all friendships.
You think you're only going over for a drink,
or dinner, or a party,
and suddenly sex is presented as an option
on the menu
that was never an option before,
and if you choose it,
you lose
and if you don't choose it,
you lose...

This is not a poem about Magali
or men
or women...
This is a poem about sex.
Sex is Mahakali, the great consort,
controller of time and death,
the force of anger...

Magali was angry tonight...
I don't blame her.
The German was an asshole
in the way he treated her...

But here's my confession:
If Magali was in my apartment,
I'd make a play for her, too.
I can't help myself.
I'm just a man,
subject to the same forces,
But still,
I have manners.
No one can sleep on a loveseat.
My bed is big enough for two.

I WILL MISS ALL THAT WHEN I'M GONE

I like watching the large birds float high in the sky.
I don't know what kind of birds they are
but they have these huge wingspans
and they make flying seem so effortless.
I sit out on my tiny balcony in the morning
drinking my coffee and watching them.

I usually have an apple croissant with my coffee
first thing in the morning.
I buy one every day at the corner store
just so I can eat it first thing the next morning
with my first cup of coffee
out on my tiny balcony
watching the birds that float so high in the sky.
I look forward to my apple croissant and my coffee each
morning.
It's these little rituals that keep life orderly.

I wonder where the birds go when they leave the sky.

THE GHOST OF MIKE MOON

Mike Moon died in this apartment in 1939.
I moved in in 2019.
But what's 80 years to a ghost? A blink of an eye?
He wanders through these walls at night,
coughing and hacking, keeping me awake,
wanting to tell me stories... like,
about the time he and Billy Sutton stole a car
and outran the state police and local sheriff,
or when he went to prison for growing marijuana
but got paroled out early for saving a guard's life
during a prison riot,
or the time he got caught in bed with his mom's best friend.
I pull the pillow over my head.
I don't want to hear his stories.
Everybody's got stories,
especially the dead.
In fact, the dead are nothing but stories.
And I've already had enough of living people's stories
without some ghost sitting on the edge of my bed saying,
"Did I ever tell you about the time I married my cousin?"
"Yeah, Mike," I reply, "about fifteen times."
But he launches into it anyway
Just like the living do...
just like you do
and just like I do.
It's as if our lives don't matter
unless we can turn it into a story.
I suppose that's why we do it –
because our lives don't matter.

At any rate, the exorcist comes next week.
Maybe then I can get some sleep.

TREMOR

A small tremor rolled through town today,
probably not even a 4 on the Richter Scale.

We get them quite often on this isthmus.
The land is stretched so thin,
pulled apart as it were,
by North and South America
going their opposite ways
geologically and geopolitically...
One of these days, this bridge will just snap,
and we'll all be flung into the sea.
But it was just a small adjustment today,
just a minor release of pressure...
It shook my door frame for a second,
And then moved on.

I'll refrain from the obvious metaphors
about love,
about how love used to strike suddenly,
like a 9.0 mega-quake,
completely destroying my world.
And I'll avoid the overused reference
to the earth moving beneath my feet.
And I don't need to draw attention
to the obvious fact
that all I can expect
these days
are minor releases of pressure...

No, it was just a small tremor.
It happened and then moved on,
just as I have.

CURTIS

Curtis joined us for dinner last night.
He's not going to make it much longer.
Four old gringos out for the evening
at the Latino version of the Sizzler.
"I'm going to lose weight," he said
after he ordered a double order of mashed potatoes.
"I need to lose weight," he repeated,
patting his huge stomach.
He could barely make it from the car
to the restaurant.
But it's not his weight – it's his lungs. They're shot.
Years of smoking... and he still sneaks a smoke
when he thinks we're not looking.
When we drove back to our apartment building,
he had to rest against the car
before attempting the six steps up to his room.
He uses an oxygen machine at night
and coughs all day.
He's not going to make it much longer.

Death likes our little apartment building.
It's full of old gringos like Curtis
and Bob and Fred
and me.
Death swings by when he needs to make his quota.
Easy pickings here,
like shooting fish in a barrel.
Mike went a few months ago, down in room number three,
two doors down from Curtis's room.
The police and the coroner know the routine here,
and they carried Mike out quietly.

They say everyone has their own fascinating history,
but all I know about Curtis is that he ran a KFC
back in the States before he retired
and moved down here
to die
south of the border.

A VERY SHORT STORY

I met you at some party.
It must have been three or four years ago.
I didn't know the host or hostess
but they were friends of my brother and his wife
so I came along for the free wine and snacks.
Everyone knew everyone, except me,
so I talked with you.
I explained that I live in Panama,
but I was visiting my brother for the holidays.
You said you had surfed in Costa Rica.
We talked about Central America.
We talked about your job
as a distribution rep for a large cheese company
and how you got to travel for your job
and how you liked that
because you liked to travel.
We talked about places you had been
and places I had been.
We talked about all the different cheeses
and different wines we both liked.
We talked about surfing and dangerous riptides.
Before I left, I gave you my card and said
to call me the next time
you were in Central America.
I never heard from you, of course.

ADVICE FOR DATING OVER FIFTY

No one likes a curmudgeon.
All the dating advice columns say this.
Spruce up your wardrobe.
Get a new haircut style.
Clean your apartment.
Get your teeth whitened.
Remember to compliment her.
Pay for dinner.
Don't be pushy.
Never talk politics on the first date.
Swipe right on everyone.
Trim your nose and ear hair.
Only one spritz of cologne.
Join a gym.
Join meet-up groups.
Dress nice.
And above all,
act natural!

PAST ITS PRIME

The label indicates a noble pedigree,
a rich history, good cultivation...
Clearly no expense was spared in
getting it to this point.
I remember when this vintage came out.
It held such promise,
but now, well... it's aged well,
but it's past its prime.
See here how the cork is dry and brittle.
That's not a good sign.
But the aroma is promising.
There's an undercurrent of warm summers,
rich soil, lush memories...
A lot of love went into this wine,
But I also get notes of regret, sadness,
maybe a hint of a dark melancholy.
That often happens with a wine that's left
on the shelf too long –
or maybe some errors were made
in how it was cared for...
See how the tannins have taken on
a leathery appearance
that mutes the color and sparkle it once had.
But that's natural,
and usually doesn't affect the taste.
Yes, bring two glasses, and let's find out.
Ah, yes. See how the first impression is quite reserved,
how it seems to hold something back?
But hold it on your tongue a moment
and feel how it blossoms full and rich
before quickly fading away,
like a flower that only blooms for one day...
and then the swallow has that slight bitterness
that comes from aging too long,
being past its prime.
It's a shame really.
It was such a good wine in its day.
Well, we might as well drink it.

LOST LOVE

All loves are lost loves,
when you think about it.
The one that got away
describes everyone you ever cared about.
Not that they were perfect
but for a moment, just for a moment,
they were perfect.

And then the moment changed
and they slipped away.

Perfection exists in the potential,
the potential of someone
to be perfect
either you
or the other person.

All loves are lost loves.

ISFET

All the rivers that run into the sea,
how do you tell them apart?
When the tsunami comes,
the ocean moves as one.

All the heavy villages built
on the side of the volcano,
when the lava comes,
which side will collapse?

All the buyers and sellers
and inside traders,
millions of them every day,
when the market falls,
who really decided?

No wonder the ancients
worshipped the God of Chaos.

PRAYER CARDS

When I was a child, on Sundays in church,
people would fill out prayer cards,
and the preacher would read them aloud,
asking for the congregation's prayers.

Maybe they still do that in small churches.
I don't know.
I stopped going to church years ago.

But now I read the comments
to the "healing music" videos on YouTube,
and it seems about the same.

"My son is in ICU at the Aurora General Hospital…"

"At this point of my life, I am in a very bad situation
because of some bad choices I made…"

"Last year I had major surgery on an aneurysm.
The recovery of the surgery was hard, very hard…"

"I'm 6 months pregnant
with my baby girl. I've been homeless
and have been going through so much
through my entire pregnancy…"

"Please send a distant healing
to my 9-month-old son. He just survived dengue
without having any blood transfusions
but still has high fevers…"

"I suffer from Hyperacusis (pain from sound)…"

"I have arthritic pain in both of my knees
and when I get up from sitting,
I can barely walk…"

I remember sitting in the stiff wood pews
in church, listening to the preacher read
all those cards... I was very young, but I thought,
there's so much suffering in this world.
Maybe that's why he read them out loud,
to remind us of how much people suffer.
It's almost unbearable how people suffer.

At least the people in my congregation
got to hear their words read out loud.
At least they got to see
other people bow their heads
and acknowledge their suffering.
Maybe the prayers helped—I don't know,
but at least their suffering was acknowledged.

When you type your pain
into the comment section of a computer
and send it out to the ethernet void,
how is your suffering acknowledged?

Pain is only bearable when it's acknowledged.

CONSEQUENCES

Uhhh good morning... oh God my head
I apologize for anything I said
Hand me my hat and walking cane
I need some coffee and a brand-new brain
Where's my belt? Where's my shoes?
Where did I get this tattoo?
Uhhh good morning... I'm in such pain
I remember your face but not your name
I remember holding someone soft
And doing things with our clothes off
But I woke up on your kitchen floor
I need more coffee then I'll hit the door
Uhhh good morning... I'm in such a fog
Is this your house? Is that your dog?
And who is this? Is this your child?
We drank all that? We went hog wild?
Where's my hat? Where's my car?
You say we walked here from that bar?
I need some coffee; I need a new life
Just what the hell will I tell my wife?

AÑEJO

Gone are the days when we needed more tequila
and you and I decided to drive to the liquor store,
and it was the dead of winter, snow everywhere,
and I decided to ride on the outside of your car
standing on the running boards, holding on tightly
while you drove feverishly and the snow fell
and we made it to the liquor store and back
with our fresh bottles of cheap tequila
and never saw a cop, and the party went on
and everyone danced and drank...

Tequila, they say, is the devil's drink.
It makes you do things you wouldn't normally do.
Thank God I did those things when I was young.
If I buy tequila now, I only buy Añejo
for I know the true price of a hangover.

But I have this memory, you see.
You and I were making margaritas for this party
with tequila and salt and lime
and we were drinking while we were mixing
and the night was wonderful
and we were drunk
and we ran out of tequila
but the party was in full swing
so we needed more tequila, you see,
so obviously you and I needed to go to the store
and buy more tequila
and the night was dark and cold
but you had this old VW bug with running boards...
I don't know how we did it.
We were both so drunk.
You drove and I rode shotgun on the outside.
I don't remember the year, but it had to be
at least forty or fifty years ago...
Can you imagine now? DUI, double DUI...

years of probation and fines and loss of license.
But it was Chicago and we were young.
We were so fucking young,
and we managed to pull it off
without being caught.
You were living with this artist
but she was moving to Africa to paint.
I think that's what the party was for.
It was a going-away party.
And there was a certain sadness in you
because you knew this was the end,
the end of the relationship with her.
But you decided to keep a brave face
but a brave face needed tequila,
and so I set up a small table in your apartment
and we invited all of your friends
and all of her friends
and we made margaritas at this table
and handed them out to everyone,
drinks to celebrate her move to Africa
like it was some job promotion,
although it was really like a termination.
And I made strong margaritas
and the music played loud
but then we ran out of tequila
and I shouted at you over the music,
"We need more tequila."
And we got our coats and hats without a word
because we knew what had to be done
and we were drunk but you had a car
and the liquor store wasn't that far of a drive.
I don't know why I decided I needed to ride
on the outside of the car.
Maybe I hoped the fresh air would clear my head.
Tequila has a way of clouding your thinking.
And cheap tequila has a way of fucking you up.
We were lucky there were no cops.
We were lucky we didn't kill ourselves
or someone else.

I don't drink much tequila these days,
and if I do, I only drink Añejo tequila.
That's tequila that's pure agave azul and aged for a year
in an oak barrel. It will still knock you on your ass
but you won't be so poisoned the next day.

I don't remember your lover's name...
I want to call her Kay,
but I'm not sure that was it.
She was a good artist, pure and intense,
and she painted elephants and bones
on huge canvases.
It's hard to love an artist.
You have to be subservient to their art
even moreso than they are.
I remember she had this translucent skin
and ultra-blond hair,
and you with your red Irish hair and genes...
It was a doomed love affair.
And I knew you were sad
but I knew it had to end
and you knew it had to end
because she had to follow her art,
and so you decided to throw a party,
a true Irish wake
but with tequila,
because nothing numbs the pain faster
than tequila
which is why I drink it now.
It numbs the pain of looking back at memories
like this one
when we were all so young, so incredibly young,
and hopeful, and stupid, and loud, and drunk,
and so wonderfully alive.

BIG HOUSES ARE LONELY PLACES

I like to play the lottery,
not because I think I have a chance in hell of winning,
but because I like to dream.
You know the dream. We all have it:
"What would you do if you won millions of dollars?"
It's the best dream ever—well worth a dollar.
But it occurred to me today:
What would I really do if I won millions of dollars?
Buy a big house in the country?
No, because I would be far away from my friends
and no one would visit me.
Big houses are lonely places.
Buy a RV and travel?
No, because—again—it would be lonely.
Driving for long distances is fatiguing,
no matter how pretty the view.
Buy a fancy car and designer clothes?
No, because that just makes you a target for robbery.
I really have very limited choices for what to do
if I won millions of dollars. And why is that?
Because right now I have the perfect life:
I rent a small studio apartment at a reasonable price.
I don't need a car. I can walk to the gym,
or to the grocery store, or to the liquor store,
or to see my friends. The climate is good here.
I don't need anything else.
But my mind persists:
But what if you DID win millions?
What would you do
if you could do the thing you enjoy doing most?
I have thought about this for many years
and here is my honest answer:
If I was suddenly very very very rich,
I would first find the best doctors I could
and get a complete physical check-up,
the best that money could buy,

because I want to live to enjoy my new wealth.
Then I would have my teeth whitened
so I looked better.
And I would get a better haircut.
I would rewrite my will.
I would set up trust funds for the people I care about.
And then...
And then...
And then I would travel first class and visit
every brothel and bathhouse and sex club
in the world (when it was safe to travel, of course)
because that is the thing I really enjoy doing most.

Now I know what you're thinking:
How does that make me any different than
Jeffrey Epstein?
Well, I wouldn't be doing anything illegal.
I would stick with consenting adults.
There's enough of them around.
But other than that difference,
there is none. Let's face it, men are just dogs.

But luckily, I will never have to find out
exactly how depraved I am
because I will never win the lottery.

It's easy to be good
when you can't afford to be bad.

NOBODY KNOWS

Nobody knows how you've suffered,
what you've gone through in your life,
and nobody will ever know.
That's just the way it is, kiddo.
Nobody knows how anyone has suffered.
And nobody knows the heights you've reached,
the depths you've felt,
the love you've found,
or the love you've lost.
That's just the way it is.
At least, that's what I think.
But it's been so long since I've been in love
that I could be wrong.
Only love lets you see.
Only love makes you strong.
I got an email this week
that my first wife had died.
We hadn't talked in twenty years.
Go make a poem out of that.
If you live long enough, you will outlive
those you love,
and then some will outlive you.
That's just the way it is.
Live long enough and you will be forgotten,
but until then, you will be unforgiven.
Go make a poem out of that.
That's just the way it is.
Nothing amounts to much,
and nobody knows how you've suffered,
or how much you're still trying
to get it right.

TIME TRAVEL MAKES FOR PAINFUL LESSONS

Some people are like black holes,
distorting space and time around them
as they suck you in with their beauty,
their mystery, their intelligence,
their sexuality,
their very nature...
And where you start out is not where you
end up.
Because of their gravitational pull,
you are spun out of control,
into your own past.
You travel back in time
to a younger you.
And after the affair is over
you end up stuck in the past
of the you who started that affair.
This distortion of time and space
leaves you not knowing how to love,
not knowing how to sex,
not knowing anything,
older and younger at the same time.
And then you learn
to avoid such persons in the future.

All black holes are beautiful
from a distance.

BEAUTY

She was so beautiful,

for whatever beauty is worth,

which isn't much.

Here's a photograph
taken maybe six or eight years ago.
See how beautiful she was.

I loved her.

I have no idea where she is now.

I hope she's still beautiful,
but it's no concern to me now.

She left my friend to sleep with me
and I found out later that while
she was seeing me, she was also sleeping
with another guy.

See what I mean?

THE ONLY ONE

All of the bathhouses in the world
are closed
due to the pandemic.
Well, not all.
There's one in a sketchy area of San José
that's open.
As soon as I get vaccinated, I'm going there.
But the rest of the bathhouses
in the rest of the world?
All closed.
All over the world.
Places I used to call home.
In Amsterdam, Madrid, Lisbon, Frankfurt,
Portland, Denver, Chicago, Reno...
all closed.
Wonderful places, full of steam, naked men,
dark corners, tiny rooms... all closed.
If there are no bathhouses to travel to,
then there's no point in traveling,
assuming, of course, that one could travel,
which one can't,
because of the pandemic.
How this one place in San José has managed
to stay open, I don't know.
Maybe they bribed the health department,
who knows?
But their Facebook page says they're open,
and I'm going there
as soon as I get vaccinated.

How amazing is this?
That I live in the one city
in the whole wide world
that has an open bathhouse... amazing!

GIGGLES

I play the lottery.
just for giggles now,
because I know I'll never win
the big jackpot.
The odds are just
too gigantic.
You might as well swim
in a tsunami.
Eventually you figure out
that life is just another lottery.
You spend years playing,
hoping, dreaming of sudden wealth,
dreaming of sudden transformation
dreaming of deus ex machina change,
until the day you realize that
you'll never win the big one.
And after that,
you just play for fun,
for giggles.
See the girl at the end of the bar?
Wanna chat her up?

Why bother?

Why not?

LIFE

I am convinced that life is just a dream.
I know life seems long,
but that's only because you're in the dream,
this dream of life
And when you wake up,
you will find yourself home
in a world you cannot even imagine now,
and you will wake up
and look back on this life,
and you will say to yourself,
"What a strange dream."

OPINIONS AND ASSHOLES

Ever see the monkeys at the zoo
throw their own shit
at the gawking spectators?
That's mankind, buddy.
That's the human race.
They drop out of trees
grab their opinions out of their ass
and throw them at you
with all their strength.

Look at the person next to you,
or the next person in the street,
their hands smeared with
condescending judgments.
They stink of stupid thoughts,
so proud of their creation,
so proud they can repeat
something they heard
from some other monkey,
just waiting for the chance
to smear it all over you.

I'm not trying to be negative.
I'm just telling you how it is.
Opinions and assholes — everyone's got one.

WAITING FOR SOMETHING

I am waiting for ten o'clock.
I have to take the bus to Escazú
this morning to see my doctor
again.
Getting old gets old.
He will check my heart
again.
I will wonder how much longer
I will live
again.
Maybe he'll adjust my medications.
I don't seem to care anymore.

Fifteen more minutes until I leave.
I think about the many questions
he will not ask me:
"Are you seeing anyone?"
"When was the last time
you were with a woman?"
"What do you do with your time?"
But I know I am the only one who asks
these questions.

I spend all my time waiting.
Then something happens.
And then I wait again.
The waiting gets longer.
The somethings get shorter.
Getting old gets old.

RESTING ON MY LAURELS

I don't know if I have any more books
in me.
Maybe I've said all I have to say.
Life is pointless; you age; you wait;
people are stupid; things don't work out;
but occasionally there is sex.
That about sums it up, don't you think?

I used to paint.
One day I just stopped.
I used to write books.
Maybe I've just stopped.
Or maybe I'm just resting.
I've never been able to force writing.
It just comes when it comes.
It's a lot like sex that way.
Suddenly someone appears
and then one day they just disappear.
Life is like that too, I guess.
Maybe I just getting ready to disappear.
I'm just doing it in stages.

WHAT HAPPENED TO YOU?

What happened?
Did you become successful at work?
Did you become secure in your decisions?
Did you come to believe your opinions?
Come to believe that you knew
what was best for other people?
You used to listen.
You used to pause before you spoke.
Now you ignore everyone
and just announce how things will be.
You're no longer fun.
It's all just about you.

The sad thing is,
you will never know why you ended up alone.
People are not honest.
I am not honest.
I will just disengage,
like everyone else,
and move away
slowly at first,
but eventually I will not be your friend,
just like everyone else.
"Tapering" is what we used to call it.
And you will never know
what happened to you.

And one day you will say,
"Whatever happened to Ricardo?"

ONCE IN A WHILE

Every once in a while
you have to let yourself go to seed.
Just, you know, to replenish the soil
from which you spring.

Don't try to reinvent yourself;
Just let nature take its course.
See what you become
after a fallow season:
gnarly overgrown dank bog
or craggy weather-beaten cliff.

See what you've become
without society's manicured conditioning.

Just let yourself go for a season.

Don't worry:
You can always spruce up next year.
You always do clean up nice.

NEED OVERRIDES EVERYTHING

Remember the time you had that sore throat?
And you said, "I don't take antibiotics
because they're not natural..."
And so you did a cleansing or some bullshit
and drank a lot of green tea
and the sore throat turned into strep throat
and you couldn't swallow because of the pain
and so you ran to the clinic begging for penicillin?

Or remember the lecture you gave us
about how a real man doesn't run after a woman,
how a real man needs to stay in charge?
That no pussy was worth losing your dignity?
And then you met her
and drunkenly texted her night after night
begging her to take you back...

Or remember the time you said that
controlling illegal immigration was easy?
That you could just build a wall...
Until you looked out at the vastness
of millions of starving refugees
with no home to go back to
and nothing left to lose,
and you watched helplessly as they
tore down the gates of your precious philosophy.

WHO WOULD I TELL?

I have to write
if I want to survive.
It's not that I have no one to talk to;
It's more that the things I have to say
I can't tell anyone...
but I can write them down.
Like the beautiful girl in the pool
who asked me if I wanted her.
I thought she liked me,
but then when we got to my room
and took our clothes off,
she said, "You know, women cost money."
Turns out she was a hooker.
She must have sized me up
as a typical stupid old gringo.
Or how about the psycho-killer in my room
the night before, who kept calling me
"Daddy" as he ate my ass?
Or my late-night dip in the hot tub
with a gay couple from Atlanta
and me holding each of their cocks
in my hands as they touched me?

And all of that was just in one weekend.
Who could I tell these things to?
Who would believe me?
Who would not judge me?

MATING SONG

The crickets start when the rains stop,
usually in the early evening.
They say that crickets rub their legs together
to make their mating song.
I assume it's a mating song they're making.
Why else sing?

I wonder if crickets will mate
with any partner who shows an interest?
I used to be like that.
If a potential partner was willing, I was ready.
But lately, I've become more discerning.
And by "lately" I mean the past decade.
And by "discerning" I mean solitary.
Or maybe there are just less crickets around
to answer my song.

Of course, I live in a small town…
That limits the choices.
And I've aged considerably…
That further limits the options.
In fact, to be honest, the only option
is the brothel in the next town.
And I don't even make it over there
that often any more.

All of which raises the existential question:
If the only option is a brothel
in the next town,
why bother singing at all?

And yet, still I sing.
I'm a solitary cricket on a dark night
in a small town,
doomed by time, my genetics, desire,
and my inability to not repeat my mistakes.

THE EXPAT CAME TO PERU

The expat came to Peru
to try ayahuasca.
He had money.
He wanted that transcendental experience.
He had the right connections.
He found a shaman.
He did the ceremony.
And in the ceremony, he discovered
how the inner and the outer were one,
how his skin was the same as the oxygen
that wraps around planet Earth,
how the song of the elephant and the turtle
are the same,
how the trees sing to each other,
how the light from God is all around us,
how time flows both forward and backwards
at the same time,
how our ignorance blinds us,
how life is eternal,
how every moment is perfect,
and how incredibly blessed we are to be here...

The next afternoon, when he awoke,
his head hurt something terrible,
and he was extremely thirsty,
and on his way to get water from the sink,
he stubbed his toe on the leg of the table,
and he had a difficult time stopping the bleeding
but he finally managed to bandage his toe
with tape from his first aid kit.

THE "WHAT I'VE LEARNED" KOAN

As I embark on my eighth decade,
people ask me, "What have you learned
from your time on this silly planet?"
And I tell them, "I've learned three things:
First, that people don't change.
They say they're going to change,
but they don't.
They promise they will change,
but they won't.
And so, I save myself a lot of time
by not trying to change people.
Second, that people don't want advice.
They say they want advice,
but they don't.
They ask for your advice,
but they don't listen.
They thank you for your advice,
but they never take it,
and that's because of rule number one:
that people don't change.
So I save myself a lot of time
by not giving advice.
And the final thing I've learned
is that there are real-world consequences
to everything you do,
and that you will probably—
if not certainly—get hurt,
no matter what you do.
And the only question is,
how much will you suffer,
which is another way of saying
that the only question is:
How stupid will your mistakes be?
By the way, see how your mind wanders
even as you read this?
You're not really listening to me, are you?

ACHING TO FLY

The time in metamorphosis is the worst.
You are changing into something beautiful,
but right now, you're stuck inside a cocoon,
unable to move, unable to interact...
All you can do is wait.
You will be beautiful.
You will spread gorgeous wings.
You will taste the sweet nectar of love again,
but all that will happen after you emerge
from this time in solitary confinement
shrouded in cotton strands of time that bind.
There's nothing you can do but wait
while nature takes its course
and changes you into a beautiful creature.
There's nothing you can do but wait.
You're right on schedule,
more than halfway there.
I know you are aching to fly,
but right now, you have to be still.
There's nothing you can do but wait.
The time in metamorphosis is the worst.

A FRIEND IN NEED

"My life's in ruins," he said.
"I understand," I said.
"I have nothing to look forward to," he said.
"That's true," I agreed.
"I have no reason not to drink every night," he said.
"Can't argue with that," I replied.
"I'm out of money," he said.
"I gotta go," I said.

I don't mind a little existential despair,
but I'm not paying for his drinks.
Misery loves company.
Poverty drinks alone.

FREE WILL

I'm just waiting for someone
to tell me what to do...
or for the heavens to give me a sign...
or for events to open an opportunity.
We think we have free will,
but we don't.
We're ticks on the edge of a leaf
waiting for a passing dog
to brush against us
so that we can hop on
for a free meal.

I'm waiting for someone
to tell me what to do,
to make me an offer I can't refuse,
to brush up against me
in a seductive way
so I can hop on
for a free meal
and a warm body
to lie with.

Free will doesn't exist.
Life is just a big dog
walking by
and we're all just ticks
hanging on the tips of leaves
waiting for our chance.

WANTON BOYS

Curtis saw his doctor today.
Nothing but bad news.
You can't make a poem
out of a cancer diagnosis.

"As flies are to wanton boys,"
the Bard wrote,
"are we to the gods—
they kill us for sport."

When life hands us crappy options
you just make crappy choices,
and so Custis is going with surgery.
They'll cut out his bladder and his prostate,
and he'll wear a bag to piss in.

Bob asked him if he'll still
be able to go to the whorehouse.
Curtis said of course he would,
but I don't think he understands...
and the whores, well...
they have better options.

But I don't expect him
to make it through the surgery.
He's got congestive heart failure,
bad lungs, is obese and smokes.
Not the best candidate for survival,
but easy picking for wanton boys
who like to pull the wings off of flies
before burning them with matches.

WAITING

It's raining.
I'm stuck inside another hotel room,
waiting for an appointment
or a meeting
or time to leave for something
it doesn't matter
I'm waiting.
That's the only time I'm alive
is when I wait.
When you're doing something,
you're in motion,
and when you're in motion
you're not conscious.
It's only when you have to wait,
when you have to do nothing,
that you are aware,
that you are truly aware.
I am listening to Christmas music
playing softly on my laptop.
I like Christmas music (not the words)
and I am thinking of someone
whom I love,
who is not mine,
who is not with me.
That's the best kind of love, don't you think?
I keep the best thoughts of her.
The worst of her is someone else's problem.
I am waiting.
I am thinking of the meeting I have to go to
in a few hours.
There I will have to interact with humans.
I do not like interacting with humans
but it's something one has to do.
I am down to my last sips of coffee.
The coffee in this hotel room is bad.

All hotel coffee is bad,
but I drink it anyway.
I look at my notes for the meeting.
It won't take very long,
and then I will do something else
and then something else
and then I will return to this hotel room
to an empty coffee cup
and I will turn on my laptop,
play more Christmas music,
and think of those that I love,
and wait for the next thing to happen.

GATO VIEJO, RATA TIERNA

"Where are you from?"
the waitress asked me as she brought me
my second glass of wine.
"Costa Rica," I answered.
"Nice," she said. "You live alone?"
"Yes," I answered. "And you?"
"I have a daughter," she said, "and we
live with my parents and my brother."
"I see," I said.
"What do you do?" she asked.
"I'm a writer. I'm retired," I said.
"I see," she said.
We both paused to size each other up.
An old cat and a tender rat,
each of us looking for a free ride.

THE SADDEST THING I EVER HEARD

They were married for almost fifty years,
but then his wife died.
A year later, their son died.
He is all alone now.
He wrote a short letter to me
and said, "All my tomorrows are gone."

THE FUCK POEM

That fuckin' fuck tried to fuck me,
but I fuckin' fucked him up fuckin' good.
He's a fuckin' asshole.
But then the fuckin' cops showed up.
I explained that we were just fuckin' around,
and then I said something fuckin' stupid.
I was fucking ripped on some fuckin' shit.
I fucked up because I stopped giving a fuck.
I wasn't fuckin' thinking
about what fuckin' mattered,
and now I'm in fuckin' jail.
Fuck.
It seems that half the fuckin' time I'm fucked;
and the other half I don't have a fuckin' clue.
I'm just fucked.
I don't have fuckin' time for this.
When I get out, I'm going to get fucked up.
I could use a good fucking.
I need to get fucked up
and do some fuckin' fucking.
I need to get fucked.
I'm so fucked.

JUST A DREAM

What if it's all just a dream?
What if I'm lying in some hospital bed
hooked up to tubes and machines,
deep asleep on meds,
dreaming of sitting here in this restaurant
surrounded by phantasm friends
swirling around me
clanking dishes, raising glasses to toast
our marvelous evening together
sharing the delight of our company,
while the cooks cook and the waiters
rush about in a swirl of airy color and mist?
Doesn't it make more sense that it's all a dream?
The way nothing is connected?
The way the moments just shift
into some new moment?
The way that it's all out of your control?
The way that life just happens to you?

Well... I guess... if life is just a dream,
you might as well
dream the best you can.

ABOUT THE AUTHOR

Robert Rahula was born in Spain to an American father and Spanish mother, but grew up in Virginia on the farm of his paternal grandparents. He returned to Menorca, Spain, in the 1960s to pursue his writing career. Over the past thirty years, Robert has published dozens of books of prose and poetry in Spain and in the United States. Readings of his poems appear on his YouTube channel, his Facebook page, and his website robertrahula.com. He travels Europe, Central and South America for several months a year, giving readings and lectures, and spends the rest of his time writing.

www.ingramcontent.com/pod-product-compliance
Lightning Source LLC
Chambersburg PA
CBHW071912070526
44583CB00016B/1951